A Guidebook to Lighthouses in South Carolina, Georgia and Florida's East Coast

RUDY KAGERER

LIGHTHOUSE ENTERPRISES, INC.
ATHENS, GEORGIA

First Edition, August 1985
Copyright © 1985 by Rudy Kagerer
All Rights Reserved

Library of Congress Catalog Card No. 85-50332
ISBN 0-933549-00-8

Price per copy: $6.95

Lighthouse Enterprises, Inc.
P.O. Box 6361
Athens, Ga. 30604

I dedicate this book to my family
and especially to my wife,

DORIS EMMA KAGERER

THE LIGHTHOUSE KEEPER'S LAMENT

Oh, what is the bane of a lightkeeper's life,
That causes him worry and struggle and strife,
That makes him use cuss words and beat at his wife?
                    It's Brasswork.

The devil himself could never invent,
A material causing more world-wide lament,
And in Uncle Sam's service about ninety percent,
                    Is Brasswork.

The lamp in the tower, reflector and shade,
The tools and accessories pass in parade,
As a matter of fact the whole outfit is made,
                    Of Brasswork.

From pillar to post, rags and polish I tote,
I'm never without them, for you will please note
That even the buttons I wear on my coat
                    Are Brasswork.

I dig, scrub and polish, and work with a might.
And just when I get it all shining and bright,
In comes the fog like a thief in the night.
                    Goodbye Brasswork.

Oh, why should the spirit of mortal be proud,
In the short span of life that he is allowed,
If all of the lining in every dark cloud
                    Is Brasswork?

And when I have polished until I am cold,
And I'm taken aloft to the Heavenly fold,
Will my harp and my crown be made of pure gold?
                    No, Brasswork.

CONTENTS

ERRATA

Page 24. Picture caption should read "Haig's Point" rather than "Bloody Point"

Pages 59-60. INDEX. The entire Index is off by 7 pages. To find indexed items, add 7 to the page given. i.e. Key West, listed as page 43, is on page 50.

* These lighthouses, of iron pile construction, are off the coast of the Florida Keys. They were not written up in this volume since they were well described and discussed by Love Dean in her fine volume "Reef Lights: Seaswept Lighthouses of the Florida Keys," published by the Historic Key West Preservation Board in 1982.

INTRODUCTION

Those who love the sea and the shore seem to find a mystic beauty in the old lighthouses that once provided the only means for a seaman to know when he was approaching dangerous water. The romantic literature and considerable legend adds to the draw of these tall standing, and in some cases, crumbling structures.

In this guidebook, I have tried to share some of the flavor of the history and legend of the lighthouses that are still standing on the southern Atlantic coast of my country, as well as directions for getting to them. If I have omitted information about your favorite lighthouse, or if I have misrepresented the facts, I am sorry. If you will take the time to write me in care of the publisher, I will be sure to make any changes that are needed in future editions of this guidebook. I hope that some of you will send me tales and legends that I have not uncovered, since they provide the real romance.

Some of the lighthouses are lucky to have people who care about them, and they are being protected, restored, and proudly shown. Some of these have museums that are manned by the volunteers that share a common love for their history. Others have none of these things, and are standing alone, as they have done for many years, facing the weather, the sea, and welcoming the occasional visitor.

If you are going to visit some of the more remote lighthouses, a few words of caution are in order. Some involve hazard, and you may run into unexpected tides, wind, wildlife, underbrush and even people. Do not go to those sites alone, and when you do go, go prepared with a map, compass and supplies. Notify an official of some sort, a park ranger or a law enforcement officer, of your destination and expected time of return. Also, access to all lighthouses is not automatic. Some are in protected areas, so that prior arrangements must be made. Don't be disappointed.

I am grateful to my many friends and relatives for their enthusiasm and support. My thanks go to the U.S. Coast

Guard personnel that helped me, particularly Petty Officers Price of Tybee Station, Van Dusen of the Georgetown Light Station and Vosburgh of Hilsboro Inlet, Mrs. Bessie Wilson Dubois of Jupiter, Mrs. Billie Burn of Daufuskie Island, Mr. Fred Wichman of Charleston, Ms. Dana Myers of Athens, Ga. and Ms. Joyce Ware of the Little Cumberland Island Association, among countless others. My thanks also to my son Eric, my partner on some wild and hairy adventures, my mother (and lifelong fan) who climbed up Cape Florida lighthouse with me, and Paul Kurz, my stepfather and loyal supporter. Finally, my heartfelt thanks to my best friend, my partner and my wife, Doris, who has encouraged my dreams, supported my efforts, tolerated my idiosyncrasies and loved me anyway for almost three decades. It has been my good fortune to have as my wife the finest women from "Rabun Gap to Tybee Light."

Those who are further interested in these and other lighthouses are invited to become a part of one of the lighthouse support groups that are listed later in this book.

My fond hope is that some of you who read this book will use it to seek out these exciting places, and have the kind of experience we did in our discovery trips. Come join us, as we climb the stairs, walk the beaches, and meet the many wonderful people who, like us, are dedicated wickies.

The information in this guidebook is the sole responsibility of the author. This was fun to do, and I plan to do some more. I am serious about accuracy. If I've made an error, let me know. Share with me and I'll share with others. You know, we wickies have to stick together.

Athens, Georgia   Rudy Kagerer
1985

A BRIEF HISTORY OF AMERICA'S LIGHTHOUSES

The earliest lighthouses built on American soil were built on the coasts of the maritime powers of the original colonies. These coastal lights were constructed and controlled by local coastal authorities. They were supported by a tonnage tax on all ships entering and leaving the ports they protected. The lights were the responsibility of private contractors who maintained the buildings, hired and paid keepers, and supplied oil and other supplies, all at a fixed price.

The first lighthouse of record was built in Boston harbor in 1716 with ten more to be added by the time of independence.

When the United States government took responsibility for the navigational aids system in 1789, two more major lights had been added, both in Massachusetts, bringing the total to 13, with four more under construction.

As the country grew, the lighthouses built on its coasts and major waterways were being built and improved. The Gulf coast lights were started in 1818 with Franks Island, the Great Lakes system in 1819 with Presque Island Light, and on the west coast, due to pressure from the gold seekers, a lighthouse was built on Alcatraz Island in 1854. When Puerto Rico became a territory in 1900, 13 active lights, built by the Spanish, were taken over. One Russian lighthouse at Sitka was taken over by the Board in 1867 when the U.S. took possession of Alaska. However, there was little interest in "Seward's Folly" as the purchase was called, so that no lighthouses were built until 1902. The Lighthouse Board assumed responsibility for Hawaii's lights in 1904, and for the 5 lighthouses in the American Virgin Islands in 1919.

Administration of the lighthouses bounced around in the federal government for over 30 years after 1789, going from the Treasury Department to Commerce, to the Commissioner of Revenue, back to Treasury, etc., until 1822, when the function temporarily took root in Treasury, with the Fifth Auditor of the Treasury in charge. The Fifth Auditor, Stephen Plimpton, was a conscientious, hard working civil servant who had only two faults. He knew very little about the technical aspects of lighthouses, and was overly frugal with the taxpayer's money, a characteristic we sometimes wish for today. The results of this combination of characteristics were to increase the number of lighthouses to 331 by 1852 and to change slowly (U.S. lighthouses did not adopt the new fresnel lens until the 1840's, over 20 years after their development). In addition, many lights were undependable and poorly lit.

In 1852 the Lighthouse Board was formed, consisting of Naval officers, Engineering and Topographical experts, and civilians of high scientific attainment. The Board worked hard to bring the system of navigational aids up to world standards, and succeeded in part. However, political patronage interfered, in that lighthouse keepers were political appointees, and many had neither dedication nor expertise. In 1898, President Grover Cleveland had the Civil Service laws amended to include keepers and other employees of the service. This act laid the groundwork for the true keepers.

In 1910, the Lighthouse Board was replaced by the Bureau of Lighthouses, within the Department of Commerce. There was now one commissioner, George R. Putnam, who remained as Bureau commissioner from 1910 to his retirement in 1935. Mr. Putnam truly modernized the system of aids in the United States during this period. If there was one fault, it was that there was so much emphasis placed on thrift that some necessary maintenance was not performed.

In 1939, just prior to the 150th anniversary of federal involvement in lighthouses, President Franklin D. Roosevelt summarily abolished the old Bureau of Lighthouses, and responsibility for navigational aids was placed under jurisdiction of the Coast Guard, where that control resides today.

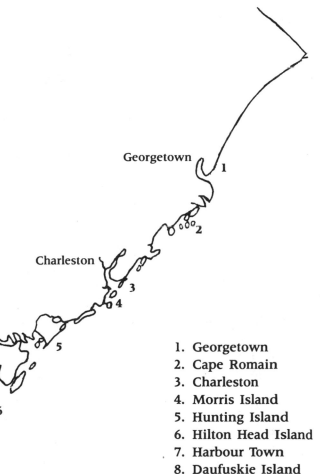

North Carolina

Georgetown

Charleston

Beaufort

Georgia

1. Georgetown
2. Cape Romain
3. Charleston
4. Morris Island
5. Hunting Island
6. Hilton Head Island
7. Harbour Town
8. Daufuskie Island

SOUTH CAROLINA

13

GEORGETOWN, S.C.

HISTORY. $5,000.00 was appropriated for this lighthouse as early as 1795, but it was not put in service until February, 1801, due to poor information and politics. The first light was a wooden structure, seventy-two feet high and twenty-six feet at the base. It burned whale oil in a six foot wide iron lantern. The first lighthouse lasted until a storm in 1806. The next one, completed in 1812, was of the same height, but constructed of brick painted white. The light was rebuilt again in 1867, as part of the post war reconstruction. It is likely that this light, like many others in the south, was destroyed by confederate raiders to prevent the union ships from utilizing its light. This time the lighthouse was built eighty-five feet high. The light is still active, and is one of the few lights that is currently manned by the Coast Guard. The light signature is 2 flashes separated by a two and seven second break. The lens are fifth order fresnel type. 124 steps lead to the top.

MUSEUM OR INTERPRETIVE SERVICE. None is known to exist at this time. A publication ". . . THAT WE SHOULD HAVE A PORT . . ." by Ronald E. Bridwell can be purchased at the Georgetown Chamber of Commerce, giving some area history.

GETTING THERE. From I-95 take exit 122 east on U.S. 521 through Manning and Andrews to Georgetown. The only way to get from Georgetown to North Island is by boat. Winyah Bay is a part of the Inland Waterway and is navigable. Boats can be launched at the Shrine launching ramp on Boulevard St. in Georgetown or at the launch ramp on South Island Road at the South Island Ferry. A map of the area may be purchased at the Chamber of Commerce. North Island is a beautiful unspoiled wildlife refuge area, with a small portion of the island allocated to the lighthouse. The rest of the island belongs to South Carolina, given by the Yawkey Foundation. Obtain permission to visit the lighthouse by calling the O.I.C. at (803) 546–5921.

TALES AND LEGENDS. There is a tale told by shrimpers, of a man with a lantern walking along the ocean beach of North Island, especially in foul weather. The keepers at one time would do so when the light went out. The Coast Guardsmen on duty also report strange happenings around the light, such as tools missing, things moved, etc. Fireman Alan Cassell, U.S.C.G. placed a cassette recorder in the lighthouse one night, and the next morning, when the tape was played back, there were unexplained noises, sounding like very weary footsteps. He claims that the sounds are not those of living human feet. What then? We can't be sure.

This is his country's guardian,
The outmost sentry of peace.

Robert Louis Stevenson

CAPE ROMAIN, S.C.

HISTORY. The first of two lights built at Cape Romain was lit in 1827. It was built on Raccoon Key, later to be renamed Lighthouse Island and made a part of the Cape Romain National Wildlife Refuge. The 65 foot tower was built on a hill to show a light 87 feet above sea level. A taller, stronger light, 150 feet high, with a first order lens was put in service in 1858. The lens and lantern room were destroyed by Confederates in 1861, but were repaired and back in service in 1866. There followed a series of cracks and foundation settling, which threw the light out of alignment, but the shifting stopped around 1891. The lighthouse continued to serve until 1947, when it was re- duced to a daymark. There are 195 steps to the top of the big tower. The stairs in the smaller tower, as well as the lantern room, are gone.

MUSEUM OR INTERPRETIVE SERVICE. None available at this time.

GETTING THERE. From I-95, take exit 86 onto I-26 to Charleston. In Charleston, pick up U.S. 17 North, and follow it to McClellanville. Once in town launch your boat at the municipal ramp or you may hire Charles De Antonio or one of his friends to take you to the island. Wear stout shoes and long pants, since the undergrowth on the island is ferocious. We could have used a machete.

TALES AND LEGENDS. There were some references to strange goings on at the lighthouse such as murders, etc., but no one seemed to be too clear on the matter.

CHARLESTON LIGHTHOUSE, S.C.
(Sullivan's Island Light)

HISTORY. A change in the channel coming into Charleston Harbor and the rapidly eroding island around the Morris Island lighthouse caused this relatively new light to be built in 1962. Uncharacteristic of lighthouses, it has an elevator as well as stairs. The tower is 163 feet high, and is triangular in cross section. The light mechanism is capable of being the most powerful light in the world, with a potential of 28,000,000 candlepower. Full power is rarely if ever used in the light. Originally orange and white, the tower is now black and white. The light shows two flashes every 30 seconds. It was fully automated in 1982.

MUSEUM OR INTERPRETIVE SERVICE. None is readily available, although the historian at Fort Moultrie kindly allowed us access to a folder full of interesting material on this light as well as the Morris Island Lighthouse.

GETTING THERE. Charleston Lighthouse is easy to reach. Drive north of Charleston on U.S. 17. Take S.C. 703 through Mt. Pleasant to Sullivan's Island. The lighthouse is on the left as you approach Fort Moultrie. You can drive very close to it, but there is a locked gate around it, as it is an unmanned location.

TALES AND LEGENDS. None known, other than a suggestion that the elevator does not always work well, and one may have to walk up and down if access can be obtained through the Coast Guard.

MORRIS ISLAND, S.C.

HISTORY. Beacons of burning pitch and oakum, large tallow candles and spider lamps were used early in Charleston Harbor to guide ships. The first lighthouse of record was begun in May 1767. It was 102 feet, base to lantern. A first order lens was installed and lit in 1858. During the Civil War, Confederate Forces destroyed the lantern and lens, and later the tower. When Federal Forces took Charleston in 1865 the harbor channels had changed  drastically. A new tower was started in 1874, 400 yards from the old site. This tower, finished in 1876, was 161 feet high with a first order lens. The tower survived a hurricane in 1885 and the Charleston earthquake in 1886, to serve until 1962, when it was replaced by the lighthouse on Sullivan's Island. The lens was sold at auction, and plans were made to destroy the tower. However, a citizen's group, led by local resident and son of a lighthouse keeper Fred Wichman and L. Mendel Rivers fought to keep it and won.

MUSEUM OR INTERPRETIVE SERVICE. None.

GETTING THERE. From I-95, take I-26 south to Charleston, picking up U.S. 17 south. Follow through Charleston, turning left (south) onto S. C. 171, to Folly Island. Turn left onto East Ashley, following it to its end at the gate of the Coast Guard Station. Park your car outside the gate, and walk to the beach outside the fence. Turn left at the beach and walk a few hundred yards. The tower is 300 yards or so from the beach.

TALES AND LEGENDS. None now known.

HUNTING ISLAND, S.C.

HISTORY. The first lighthouse was built on Hunting Island in 1859 and destroyed, probably by Confederates, around 1862. A new tower was completed in 1875 a quarter of a mile inland from the old site. This lighthouse was built of interchangeable cast iron sections that could be taken apart and put back together if necessary. The tower, 95 feet high, was lined with bricks and built upon an eight inch concrete foundation. The new complex included a three story keeper's house, an oil house and several storage buildings. By 1889 the sea had cut away the northern end of the island, causing the lighthouse to be moved again. It was moved to its current site, which is about one and a quarter miles south of the original location. By 1890 the keeper's and storage houses, dock and tram road were in operation.

The light, which had 100,000 candlepower, had a second order fresnel lens, and could be seen for 18 miles at sea. The tower is 140 feet high, with 181 steps to the top. (Beware of lighthouse leg.) Oil vapor was used for light until its retirement in 1933.

MUSEUM OR INTERPRETIVE SERVICE. There is a display area in an old storage-house that has pictures and narrative descriptions. Incidentally, the campground store sells a few items featuring the lighthouse.

GETTING THERE. From I-95, take exit 33, east on U.S. 17 to Gardens Corner, where you pick up U.S. 21 east. Simply stay on U.S. 21 through Beaufort, S.C. to Hunting Island State Park. There is a $1.00 admission fee per car.

TALES AND LEGENDS. None now known.

HILTON HEAD ISLAND, S.C.

HISTORY. A lighthouse was proposed on Hilton Head Island as far back as 1854, but the price of the land was too high. Two lighthouses were finally built on the island in 1863, with the help of Union troops then stationed at Port Royal, a forward, smaller light and a larger rear light. The rear light was blown down in 1869. The current tower was built and lit in the summer of 1881 and served until the 1930s. The brown tower is 95 feet high, with 112 steps to the top. The owners have announced their intention to renovate the lighthouse and make it a landmark for a golf course and to place it on the National Register of Historical Places. We applaud their intention.

MUSEUM OR INTERPRETIVE SERVICE. None is known at this time. Terry Bunton wrote an article about the lighthouse in the July '84 issue of "The Hilton Head Islander."

GETTING THERE. See instructions for Harbour Town Light for instructions to Hilton Head Island from I-95. The lighthouse is on private property, the Palmetto Dunes Resort. Permission may be obtained to visit the lighthouse for serious purposes by contacting the Palmetto Dunes Resort (803) 785–1161.

TALES AND LEGENDS. The awesome power of the 1898 hurricane was felt on the barrier islands of the Atlantic Coast. The keeper of the Hilton Head Light had no warning of the storm. As the storm intensified, he went to check out the light. When he did not return, his little daughter went looking for him, as the wind driven water began to rise. She found him lying dead at the foot of the winding stairs of the lighthouse. She dragged him back through the storm to the keeper's house, and spent the rest of the night dragging him up the stairs of the house an inch at a time, to keep him from the rising water. She was rescued three days later, half out of her mind from fatigue and terror. The child later became a nurse to the children of a prominent family. She remained fearful of rising tides and wind, and always wore at least one thing that was blue on her, a scarf, a belt, something. It is unclear when she died, although some suggest it may have been in the 1940's.

Two new twin keeper's houses were built at the lighthouse in the early 1940s, and two families lived there in peace until after the hurricane of 1948, when bumping, rapping sounds, slamming doors and other unexplained noises were heard in the houses. The families were glad to move out when the light was put out of service soon thereafter.

After the houses were abandoned, several people reported hearing sounds in the old houses, and one group reported seeing a lady in a blue dress dragging something up the stairs inside the house. When one of the group opened the door, the lady and her burden disappeared. The houses were moved to the area now known as Harbour Town where the Lady in Blue was seen again, or more correctly, was "felt" by three people. There have been no further reportings of the Blue Lady since the houses were renovated and converted into a delicatessen. Has she gone back to the scene of the action, the lighthouse? Will she be seen again, especially when more people go into the area to golf and vacation?

HARBOUR TOWN, S.C.
(Hilton Head Island)

HISTORY. This lighthouse, built in 1970, was the first one to be privately financed since 1817. It is the symbol of the Sea Pines Plantation. The 90 foot high red and white striped structure is on the mainland side of the island, facing Calibogue Sound and the Inland Waterway. It is open to the public daily from 8:00 am until dark. 110 steps lead to the top. The white light flashes every 2.5 seconds.

MUSEUM OR INTERPRETIVE SERVICE. None could be found, but the lighthouse sign was informative. While there, you can visit the keeper's houses which were moved from the old Hilton Head Lighthouse. These two houses have been renovated and currently house a deli a few blocks from the Harbour Town light.

GETTING THERE. From I-95 southbound, take exit 28 to S.C. 462 to U.S. 278. Northbound from I-95, take U.S. 321 south to S.C. 170 north to U.S. 278, south. Stay on 278 to Hilton Head. At Sea Pines Circle go onto Greenwood Drive a few hundred feet to the Sea Pines Security office. Purchase a one day pass for $3.00 per car. Continue on Greenwood Drive to Lighthouse Road, and to Harbour Town.

TALES AND LEGENDS. James Lawrence, a local author, wrote an article in the July 1984 "Hilton Head Islander" reporting that he and two teenage friends felt the presence of two ghosts in the old keeper's houses that are now in the Harbour Town area.

DAUFUSKIE ISLAND, S.C.

HISTORY. Daufuskie Island is a peaceful unspoiled island on Calibogue Sound a few miles north of Tybee Island, just across the sound from Hilton Head Island. Early records refer to it as "Mongin Island", named after Navy Captain John Mongin who claimed he was granted the island by King George II in 1740 for his successes against Spanish pirates.

Two sets of navigational lights were constructed on the island. One set, the Haig's Point range lights, (also referred to as the Daufuskie Island Lights), served from October, 1873 to July, 1924. The rear beacon, which was mounted on the keeper's house, had a fifth order fresnel lens. The second set, built on Bloody Point, on the southeastern tip of the Island, served from 1883 to 1922, when a Mr. Kennan bought it. The rear light here was also mounted on top of the keeper's house. Both houses are still standing, although the light has been removed from the top of the Bloody Point Light.

MUSEUM OR INTERPRETIVE SERVICE. None now available, although ex postmistress Mrs. Billie Burn was kind enough to help us with much of the information in this section. Her husband's father, Arthur Ashley Burn, was the last keeper of the Bloody Point Light.

GETTING THERE. This island is only accessible by boat. Captain Sam's Cruises run from Savannah to Daufuskie "when enough people want to go" or by charter (912) 234–7248. Vagabond Cruises run a tour from Harbour Town on Hilton Head Island daily during warmer weather. The tours visit the winery, old Union Baptist Church and the school. They have not in the past visited the lighthouses but may if enough people ask. Call (803) 842–4155 for the schedule and prices.

One can also go by private boat, since there is a public dock available. Boats can be launched at Alljoy Landing near Bluffton. The island is nine miles long and five miles wide, and not much land transportation is available. It is best to arrange for such beforehand, or be prepared for some walking.

TALES AND LEGENDS. This island was a sort of "no man's land" in the days of early settlement. During the Yemassee Indian War of 1715, in retaliation for an Indian raid on a settlement, the settlers managed to trap a group of Indians on the southeastern tip of the island, getting between them and their canoes. In the ensuing battle, all of the Indians were killed except one, who somehow escaped and swam to Tybee Island. Hence the name of the point, "Bloody Point", and the island "Daufuskie", which translated means "place of blood". The white sand today shows no signs of the violence that once took place here.

BLOODY
POINT-
REAR
RANGE
LIGHT
-1885-

Courtesy
of
Billie Burn

24

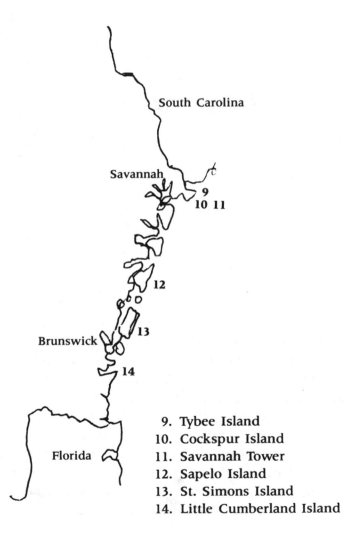

South Carolina

Savannah

9
10 11

12

Brunswick

13

14

Florida

9. Tybee Island
10. Cockspur Island
11. Savannah Tower
12. Sapelo Island
13. St. Simons Island
14. Little Cumberland Island

GEORGIA

TYBEE ISLAND, GA.

HISTORY. The phrase "From Tybee Light to Rabun Gap" has often been used to describe the State of Georgia. One of the first public structures General James Oglethorpe commissioned when he established the colony of Georgia in 1733 was a beacon to be built on Tybee Island. The tower was completed by William Blytheman in 1736. The octagonal daymark was 90 feet tall, with a 25 foot base. It was replaced in 1740 by a slightly taller tower, and again in 1757 and 1773. It was lit in 1790, with spermacetti candles.

A second order fresnel lens was installed in 1857. The lighthouse and area were occupied by Union troops during the civil war. A cannon shell from Fort Pulaski burst near the lighthouse commanders' quarters, but damage was not done until 1862, when a Confederate  force exploded a keg of gunpowder in the lighthouse, putting it out of service. It was rebuilt in 1867, with a first order lens. The first electric light was burned in Tybee light in 1933. It currently has a 750 watt white light of 30,000 candlepower, visible at night for 20 miles at sea.

The Tybee Light is 154 feet high, with 183 steps to the top. The octagonal brick tower was painted a new scheme in the 1970s. The old scheme had the lower portion painted black for 60 feet, then a white ring of 30 feet, with the remainder painted black. The current scheme is white for the first 60 feet, with the remainder dark grey.

MUSEUM OR INTERPRETIVE SERVICE. Tybee Museum, located directly across the street from Tybee Light within what was once a part of Fort Screven, is a storehouse of artifacts and other memorabilia of Tybee from the seventeenth century through the second World War, including a submarine periscope that offers a fine view of the beach and the lighthouse from inside the museum. It is open daily from 10:00 to 6:00 in the summer and from 1:00 to 5:00 in the winter. Admission is $1.00 for adults. Children 12 and under are admitted free.

GETTING THERE. From I-95, take Ga. 204 east (Abercorn St.) into Savannah. Continue to the intersection with U.S. 80 and Ga. 26, (Victory Drive). Turn right (east) and stay on U.S. 80 and Ga. 26 to Tybee Island. As you cross the bridge over South Channel, just past the Fort Pulaski National Monument, look to your left for an excellent view of Cockspur Island Lighthouse. On Tybee Island, a sign on the left will lead to the lighthouse and museum. Visitors are not ordinarily allowed in the lighthouse, but it is opened on some special occasions.

TALES AND LEGENDS. While much of the history of Tybee Light was fairly peaceful, numerous "affairs of honor" as duels were called, were fought on the grounds. Such actions often resulted in a funeral in the afternoon on one of the nearby plantations.

There is a reference to a Henry Talbot, who is said to have constructed beacons on the South Carolina and Georgia coasts prior to the arrival of Oglethorpe. That would mean that there may have been a beacon on Tybee Island before the first one reported here.

COCKSPUR ISLAND, GA.

HISTORY. The Cockspur Island Light, also called the South Channel Light, was one of two lights built to guide ships up the Savannah River past Tybee Island, around Elba and Cockspur Islands into Savannah, Georgia. The Cockspur Island Lighthouse, built on an oyster bed, has somehow survived, while the "North Channel Light", built on Oyster Bed Island, has not.

Both lights were put into service around 1848–1849. They remained in service for several years, until the Civil War, when they were both turned off. Cockspur Light was relit in 1866 and was in continuous service until 1909. It was then used as a harbor beacon until 1949, when it was permanently retired. It fell into disrepair, and was transferred to the National Park Service in 1956. The lighthouse was restored in 1978–79, and is open to the public.

MUSEUM OR INTERPRETIVE SERVICE. The lighthouse is just off the eastern tip of Cockspur Island, on which is the Fort Pulaski National Monument, where a tale of war is told in which traditional military wisdom was proven wrong. The museum and the fort offer historical insight into the area. If one asks, there is also a small amount of material on the Cockspur Island Light, as well as several other Georgia lighthouses. Admission is free in off season, costs $2.00 for adults and $1.00 for children 12 and above during the summer months.

GETTING THERE: From Interstate 95, take Ga. 204 east. It will become Abercorn St. after several name changes. Proceed into Savannah proper. Continue to the intersection with U.S. 80 and Ga. 26 (Victory Drive.) Turn right (east) and follow U.S. 80 and Ga. 26. Cross three big bridges and some smaller ones, and see Fort Pulaski National Monument on your left. Visit the monument if you wish, but continue toward Tybee Island until the next large bridge. The lighthouse is visible on the left just before you cross the bridge. You can park on the road shoulder and walk closer at low tide. (Wear shoes that can be washed.) There are several boat rentals on Tybee Island, where you can rent a small fishing boat to get to the lighthouse. The more adventurous can get to the lighthouse without a boat. You can walk from Fort Pulaski. The way is a little swampy, and you may have to swim or wade the small inlet just short of the oyster bed on which the lighthouse stands. If you are a good swimmer, you can swim from the shore near the bridge. My son Eric and I did, but decided to walk back through the swamp. By the way, that's Eric standing by the Cockspur Island Lighthouse on the front cover.

TALES AND LEGENDS. None known at this time. The ranger gave us some insight into vandalism. When they had locked the door and put glass in the lantern room, the door was often broken down, and the glass was shot out. When the lock was removed and plexiglass that would not shatter was put around the lantern room, vandalism stopped. The human mind is strange.

SAVANNAH TOWER

HISTORY. This is a very new light, as lights go. Constructed in 1964 to aid ships coming into the Port of Savannah, the light is in a tower perched on top of a white house on piles. The lantern room is 85 feet above mean sea level, and the structure sits in 50 feet of water. The word "SAVANNAH" is written in black letters on four sides and the roof, and a square red daymark is also on the sides. The light is at Latitude 31 57 north and Longitude 80 41 west, off the coast of Savannah. The light signal is a 2 white flashes every 15 seconds, with .2 second flash followed by a 2.8 second eclipse, and another .2 second flash followed by an 11.8 second eclipse. Nominal range is 25 miles.

MUSEUM OR INTERPRETIVE SERVICE. None

GETTING THERE. Follow the directions to the Tybee Island Lighthouse, and that will bring you to Tybee Island. The Savannah Light is offshore about 7 miles approximately due east of the Savannah River entrance. There are boats that can be chartered, and there are launch ramps on the island. If you do go in your own boat, be sure to take a proper navigational chart and check the weather carefully. A sudden squall can take the joy out of a day very quickly.

TALES AND LEGENDS. None now known.

SAPELO ISLAND, GA.

HISTORY. Captain Winslow Lewis built the Sapelo Island Lighthouse in 1820, installing a 15 inch reflector-type light. A fourth order fresnel lens was later added. During the Civil War Confederate Forces damaged the light, which was repaired and put back in service in 1868. A metal frame beacon was also built 660 feet away. A new beacon, built in 1877, still stands. The original lighthouse lost a battle with the sea, as the southern tip of the island eroded. It was replaced in 1905 by the present tower, which operated until the late 1920s. The lighthouse is in a state of disrepair and the keeper's house is in ruins.

1877 BEACON

MUSEUM OR INTERPRETIVE SERVICE. None now known.

GETTING THERE: Sapelo Island is owned by the State of Georgia and is administered by the Department of Natural Resources (912/485–2251). It can only be visited with permission. Tours are available. Arrangements must be made in advance through the Darien Welcome Center (call 912/437–6684). Once permission is obtained, go to the Sapelo Island Ferry dock in Meridian, Ga., which is on Ga. Rte. 99 east of I-95, to board the "Sapelo Queen" for a delightful ride to the island ($1.00). Carry your own food and water, there are no restaurants.

TALES AND LEGENDS. None now known.

ST. SIMONS ISLAND, GA.

HISTORY. The original St. Simons Island lighthouse was built by James Gould in 1808, 25 feet from the current tower. It was a white, tapered octagonal structure 75 feet tall. Initially a harbor light, it was raised to the level of coastal light in 1857 by the Lighthouse Board. It was constructed of tabby and brick, and was topped by a ten foot iron lantern lit by oil lamps that were suspended from chains. This tower was destroyed by Confederate troops in 1862 as they were withdrawing from the island.

FIRST ST. SIMONS LIGHT

The current structure was completed in 1872, after much illness among the construction crew. One of the bondsmen came onto the island to take charge when the contractor died. That bondsman also died, and a second came to oversee the finishing of the job. A third-order lens mounted at 104 feet above sea level was put into service on September 1, 1872. The lighthouse still functions automatically, showing a light that is visible for 16 miles on a clear night.

MUSEUM OR INTERPRETIVE SERVICE. In 1971 the Museum of Coastal History was opened in the keeper's house. While renovation work was being done on the lower floor, a collection of the Coastal Georgia Historical Society was exhibited on the

CURRENT LIGHTHOUSE

second floor. The eight room dwelling, fully restored, was built of "Savannah greys", greyish red brick made at Hermitage Plantation near Savannah.

The museum and lighthouse are open every day except Mondays all year. Winter hours are 1:00 to 4:00, and summer hours are 10:00 to 4:00, opening at 1:30 on Sundays. A donation of $1.00 is requested for admission to the museum, and another for the lighthouse.

GETTING THERE. This one is easy to find and visit. Take the Brunswick exit off I-95. Go through Brunswick to U.S. 17, the Coastal Highway. Bear left on U.S. 17 for a short distance and follow the signs to St. Simons Island. There is a small charge for crossing the causeway.

When you reach the island, stay on Kings Way, which changes its name to Ocean Boulevard. Stay on Ocean Boulevard until you reach the Village (a shopping area). The museum and lighthouse are one block further along Ocean Boulevard to the right. You can park in front of the museum on most days.

TALES AND LEGENDS. One Sunday morning in March 1880, the lighthouse keeper, Mr. Fred Osborne and his assistant keeper engaged in a duel on the front lawn of the keeper's house. Mr. Osborne died in the duel, and, according to legend, his footsteps on the tower steps can sometimes be heard, especially when the weather is stormy. This is apparently a friendly ghost, since no one has ever been harmed by it, as far as we know.

REFERENCES:

Historic Glimpses of St. Simons Island, 1736–1924, Coastal Georgia Historical Society, 1973.

Lighthouse, Eugenia Price, Bantam House, 1971 (Tenth Printing, 1981) A tale of James Gould, builder of the first light on St. Simons Island.

LITTLE CUMBERLAND ISLAND, GA.

HISTORY. There was early recognition of a need for a lighthouse on St. Andrew's Sound. In 1802 money was marked for construction. John Hastings of Boston finally built and lit the light in 1838. The focal plane was 78 feet above mean high tide, with a third order lens.

The light was slightly damaged during the Civil War but was never out of service during that period even though the lens was temporarily removed for safekeeping. In 1876 encroachment to the northwest of the tower accelerated. A large brick wall was built around the tower, and was filled with concrete and bricked over. The timbers and ironwork showed some decay by the late 1800's, and a new iron lantern deck was installed in 1901.

The structure was taken out of service in 1912, and was sold at auction in 1921. The Little Cumberland Island Association bought the island in 1961, allocating 10% to cottages with the rest left to wilderness. The Association renovated the light in 1968, and relit it for a short time, being forced to extinguish it because of the hazard an unofficial light presented to sea traffic.

MUSEUM OR INTERPRETIVE SERVICE. None

GETTING THERE. Little Cumberland is a privately owned and protected island. You may obtain permission to visit by writing "Little Cumberland Island Association, 4249 Dykes Dr., N.W., Atlanta, Georgia 30342." There is a public boat launch on Jekyll Island.

TALES AND LEGENDS. The light was so important during the civil war, especially with the St. Simons light destroyed, that the Union and Confederate troops took turns in the operation of the light, a rare occurrence.

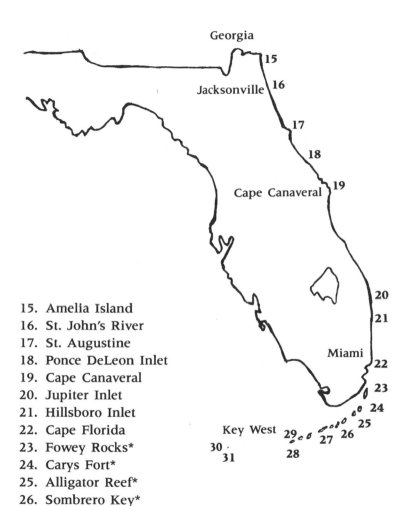

15. Amelia Island
16. St. John's River
17. St. Augustine
18. Ponce DeLeon Inlet
19. Cape Canaveral
20. Jupiter Inlet
21. Hillsboro Inlet
22. Cape Florida
23. Fowey Rocks*
24. Carys Fort*
25. Alligator Reef*
26. Sombrero Key*
27. American Shoal*
28. Sand Key*
29. Key West
30. Fort Jefferson
31. Loggerhead Key

*Not included in this book.

FLORIDA-EAST COAST

AMELIA ISLAND, FLA.

HISTORY. The first lighthouse on Amelia Island was built in 1839, as part of the coastal system of navigational aids. The cylindrical whitewashed brick tower was renovated in 1885, and again in the early 1900's.

The focal plane of the lantern is 105 feet above mean high water, even though the tower is only 65 feet high. The tower sits on a hill about two miles from the north end of the island, about one mile from Fernandina.

The lens is third order fresnel, made by Barbier and Benard of Paris, France. The lantern rotated on ball race consisting of rounded grooves riding on 12 balls which rotated by means of a clock drum which had to be rewound every four hours. The 1921 Coast Guard inspection listed an oil lamp that burned with 1500 candlepower. The light has since been electrified and automated. The light signal is a 2.5 second flash, with sectional red covering the shoal water in Nassau Sound, and white for the remainder. The white light has a nominal range of 23 miles, the red 19.

MUSEUM OR INTERPRETIVE SERVICE.   None.

GETTING THERE.   From I-95 take the second exit south of the Ga./Fla. state line onto Route A1A east. Follow A1A to Fernandina, driving south through Fernandina to Wolfe St. Turn left onto Wolfe St. to Lighthouse Circle. Lighthouse Lane is on the left from Lighthouse Circle. The road is gated, and permission to enter the property should be obtained.

TALES AND LEGENDS.   None now known.

ST. JOHNS RIVER, FLA.

HISTORY. The first lighthouse of record was built at the mouth of the St. Johns River in 1830 at a cost of $10,550.00. It was apparently undermined and another was built in 1835. Encroachment continued, and the Lighthouse Board spent money in 1853 and 1854 to secure the lighthouse. A report in 1853 describes the lighthouse as needing repair, but none was done because of a dispute over the land on which the lighthouse stood. Title to a new site was obtained in 1857, and a new tower was built in 1859.

The lighthouse was destroyed by Confederates in the early 1860's and was rebuilt and relit in 1867. The steamship lines, unhappy with the light, agitated for additional aids until the lightship from Brunswick was moved to the mouth of the river in 1929.

The third order fresnel lens showed a fixed white light 77 feet above mean high water. The red brick tower is cylindrical, and the lantern room is a 10 sided polygon.

MUSEUM OR INTERPRETIVE SERVICE. None.

GETTING THERE. From I-95 take Fla. 105 east to the Mayport ferry. Take the ferry across to Mayport. Follow U.S. A1A to the main street in Mayport, and turn left to the U.S. Naval Station in Mayport. Present your auto registration, your driver's license and proof of insurance at the visitors building. Visitors are normally allowed on the base.

TALES AND LEGENDS. None now known.

ST. AUGUSTINE, FLA.

HISTORY. St. Augustine is truly steeped in history. In 1821 the territory of Florida became a part of the United States. A harbor light, with fourth order fresnel lens was built in 1855. Confederate troops destroyed it at the beginning of the Civil War. The Lighthouse Board relit the light in 1867. Then, because of beach erosion, they built a new tower about a half mile from the old site, completing it in 1874. The keeper's house was finished in 1876. The light, whose focal plane height was 161 feet above sea level, could be seen for 18 miles. The lamps were fueled with lard oil, then kerosene. In 1936 the light was electrified, in 1955 it was automated, and in 1969 it was taken out of service.

Now, the good news. The lighthouse and keeper's house are now undergoing renovation, and a maritime museum is being planned. Deductible contributions can be sent to "Junior Service League of St. Augustine, P.O. Box 244, St. Augustine, Fla. 32084." Label them "Lighthouse Rehabilitation."

MUSEUM OR INTERPRETIVE SERVICE. Not yet, but things are looking very hopeful.

GETTING THERE. From I-95, take Fla. 16 east to St. Augustine. After entering St. Augustine, turn south onto U.S. 1, then south, onto U.S. A1A. Follow A1A to the city limits, and watch for a sign on your left that says "Lighthouse Park Fishing Pier". Take a sharp left onto Old Beach Road to the lighthouse.

TALES AND LEGENDS. None at this time.

PONCE DeLEON INLET, FLA.

HISTORY. A lighthouse tower was built at Mosquito Inlet, later called Ponce DeLeon Inlet, in 1835. It was never lit, and fell to storms and neglect. The current tower was completed and lit in 1887, after much delay. The lighthouse is 175 feet high, with 203 steel steps spiraling to the top. The light was taken out of service in 1970, and was temporarily abandoned. In 1972, the Ponce DeLeon Inlet Lighthouse Preservation Association was incorporated, and a historic monument and museum was started. A balcony around the lighthouse near the top was added, and the buildings were renovated. In 1982, a new light was installed and the light was put back into service. The red brick conical tower shows a flashing white light that can be seen for 16 miles at sea.

Photo by
Stan Mason

MUSEUM OR INTERPRETIVE SERVICE. The Association mentioned above operates the reservation, with one building housing the original lens and lighthouse artifacts, another with a museum of the sea, and yet another furnished as in 1890. There is also a ship's store which sells memorabilia. Admission is $1.50 for adults and $.50 for children, including the lighthouse. Even if you can't visit, you can send $3.00 for an Associate Membership to: Ponce DeLeon Inlet Lighthouse Preservation Association, Inc., 4931 South Peninsula Dr., Ponce Inlet, Fla. 32019. You will receive a membership card and be placed on the newsletter mailing list.

GETTING THERE. From I-95, take U.S. 92 east to South Atlantic Avenue (U.S. A1A), following it to its end, then turn left onto S. Peninsula Dr. The lighthouse complex is on your left. (Watch for the tower.)

TALES AND LEGENDS. The soap opera "As The World Turns" filmed a segment in the lighthouse. In the sequence, an actor and actress struggled at the top of the lighthouse with appropriate screaming. The local police received three phone calls reporting trouble in the lighthouse.

A local fisherman fell from his boat and the boat drifted away. He followed the light, and swam the two or so miles to shore. His comment afterward was in the nature of "The lighthouse saved my life". It was not the first time the light had saved a life.

THE LIGHTHOUSE—1934

It knows no lands, no flags, no kings,
These are inconsequential things.
The one important thing tonight,
That every seaman, black or white,
Who seeks a harbor sees a light.

We talk about world brotherhood,
But only here we make it good.
We go on building ships of war,
But, God be praised, do one thing more;
We build a lighthouse on the shore.

The lighthouse has no special friends,
No special foes, when night descends.
In all the earth the only place,
Though statesmen talk and kings embrace,
Where man becomes one common race.

—Douglas Malloch in San Francisco Chronicle
(From the Keeper's Log, Fall, 1984)

CAPE CANAVERAL, FLA.

HISTORY: The first lighthouse on Cape Canaveral, built in 1848, was inadequate, since ships had to come too close to see the light in the 60 ft. tower. A new 150 ft. tower was begun just prior to the Civil War, but was not put into service until May 10, 1868. The conical tower, built of cast iron and lined with bricks, lifted the first-order lens 137 feet above sea level. In 1873 the tower was painted with black and white horizontal bands.

Sea erosion was working against the tower, and by 1883, only 192 feet of beach remained. The Lighthouse Board had the tower moved 1½ miles inland in 1894. The light is still active, but the other structures are in ruins, and the lighthouse itself is in need of renovation. The bullseye lens can be seen for 26 miles on a clear night.

Official
U.S. Coast
Guard Photo

MUSEUM OR INTERPRETIVE SERVICE. None.

GETTING THERE. The lighthouse is on a protected military base, Cape Canaveral Air Station. In order to visit the area for legitimate reasons, such as photographing the lighthouse, permission must be obtained.

Write: Director of Public Affairs,
Eastern Space and Missile Center
Patrick Air Force Base, Fla. 32925

Request permission to visit the lighthouse, and give a primary and an alternate date.

Take S.R. 528 (Beeline Expressway) east from I-95 to the Bennett Causeway, and follow the Cape Canaveral Air Station signs.

TALES AND LEGENDS. None now known.

JUPITER INLET, FLA.

HISTORY. Designed by Lt. George G. Meade, this light was built under the most difficult of conditions. Five hundred tons of material were landed at Indian River Inlet from large sailing vessels, and lightered in shallow draft scows the thirty-five miles to Jupiter Inlet. The combination of shallow water, mosquitoes, heat and Indians caused many delays. The light was finally lit in 1860, only to be put out again in 1861, presumably by Confederate raiders who removed and hid the lens and lantern to prevent the light's use by blockading union ships.

Soon after the war ended, an agent was sent to Jupiter who found and replaced the illuminating apparatus with the help of Captain James A. Armour, who was a very competent head keeper for over forty years. The light was lit again in 1866, its first order fresnel lens shining.

The tower was left a natural brick color for the first fifty years, but became discolored due to internal dampness, and was painted with red art cement around 1910.

In 1928, the old system of weights and mineral oil lamps was replaced with electric rotating lamps. In that same year a violent hurricane hit, breaking out one of the bullseyes. The pieces were collected and the lens was repaired, being held together with iron bars, which are in place today.

The Jupiter lighthouse was recently repainted and renovated for its centenary and still operates. The light has 880,000 candlepower and can be seen for 18 miles at sea level. The tower is 105 feet tall, and is 146 feet above sea level.

MUSEUM OR INTERPRETIVE SERVICE. Not one

but two museums are available at this site for the interested wickie. There is a fairly extensive museum maintained by the Loxahatchee Historical Society in a larger building near the entrance to the lighthouse grounds. Another smaller exhibit is in a small building at the foot of the lighthouse itself (possibly the old oil storage house). Both museums and the lighthouse grounds are open to visitors from 12:00 noon to 2:30 on Sundays. Admission to both is free.

GETTING THERE. Jupiter Lighthouse is easily seen from U.S. 1. Exit I-95 to Jupiter. Turn left (north) onto U.S. 1. Turn right onto Jupiter Drive, and right into the park.

TALES AND LEGENDS. This lighthouse is replete with tales. In 1872, a roaring northeaster drove a Mallory steamer, the Victor, ashore south of the inlet. The keeper and assistant keeper sailed down the inlet, arriving in time to help bring the passengers and crew safely to shore. Among other things that the lighthouse crew acquired from the wreck were three fine dogs, named fittingly Vic, Storm and Wreck.

There was a tale of pirate treasure said to have been buried on the reservation. The loot was said to consist of gold and other valuables taken from a Mexican church. It was said that one of the pirates came back at intervals to dig up enough to satisfy his needs, then he came no more. An assistant keeper spent a great deal of his spare time digging a great hole. One night practical jokers borrowed the great iron washpot from the Captain's back yard, and buried it in the hole. The poor man was so excited when his shovel struck metal, and the disappointment he felt when he discovered the hoax was so great that he never dug in the hole again.

A third tale, one of bravery, tells of the sixteen year old son of the keeper during the 1928 hurricane. The electricity was lost, the emergency generator didn't work, so Captain Seabrook, despite an infected hand, installed the mineral lamps back into the lighthouse. His sixteen year old son, seeing his father weak and in great pain, insisted that he must go into the tower to turn the light. This he did for four violent hours, during which time the tower swayed as much as seventeen inches from the vertical. A truly courageous act, typical of the heroics of the lighthouse keepers and their families.

The Jupiter Light was also the start of the long walk to Miami made by the famous "Barefoot Mailman". (See Hillsboro Inlet for more information on the mailman.)

REFERENCES:

"Jupiter Lighthouse", Bessie Wilson Dubois, Reprinted from "Tequesta", The Journal of the Historical Association of Southern Florida, Number XX, 1960.
"Shipwreck in the Vicinity of Jupiter Inlet", Bessie Wilson Dubois, published, 1975.
(Both volumes were available at the Museum.)

So to the night-wandering sailors,
pale of fears,
Wide o'er the watery waste a light appears.
Which on the far seen mountains
blazing high,
Streams from some lonely watch-tower
in the sky.

Homer

HILLSBORO INLET, FLA.

HISTORY. This lighthouse was built to be exhibited. A Chicago steel firm built it for the Great St. Louis Exposition in 1904. When the exposition closed in 1904, the Government purchased the tower and second order fresnel lens, and moved the massive unit to Hillsboro Inlet. The job was completed and the light was lit in 1906. The early fuel was kerosene. The keepers had to carry the fuel up the 175 steps to the lantern room from storage tanks located at the bottom. The light was lit from one hour before sunset to one hour after sunrise.

This light, as many of the early lights, rotated on a mercury filled reservoir, governed by a weight hanging in a tube that ran down to the watch room. The keeper had to hand wind a drum that provided the power for the rotation every half hour. There was little time to doze or do other things while the light was operating.

The light was converted to electricity in the late 1920's, and in 1966 the light was upgraded to 2,000,000 candlepower. The lens is 136 feet above mean sea level, with a total tower height of 145 feet. Nominal range is 28 miles. The tower is described as an octagonal pyramidal skeleton tower with a central stair cylinder. The light, still operational, makes one complete revolution every 40 seconds, with one second flashes every 20 seconds. The landward side of the light is occluded.

MUSEUM OR INTERPRETIVE SERVICE. None at this time. The O.I.C. kindly gave us an information sheet on the lighthouse, from which the above information was taken.

GETTING THERE. Take exit 37 off I-95, or the Deerfield Beach exit off the Florida Turnpike. Go to U.S. A1A, turn south and follow to Lighthouse Point, which is just north of Hillsboro Inlet. Access to the area is through private property with a guarded gate. Permission can be obtained by writing to O.I.C., USCG Light Station, Hillsboro Inlet, Pompano Beach, Fla. 33062.

TALES AND LEGENDS. There is a plaque on the reservation commemorating the death in Hillsboro Inlet of James E. Hamilton, the famous barefoot mailman. He lost his life here on October 11, 1887 while attempting to cross the inlet.

A series of unexplained fires broke out in the area surrounding the lighthouse. After much investigation it was determined that the cause of the fires was the magnifying and concentrating power of the lighthouse lens. A shield was then constructed on the landward side of the light, and the problem of "lens created fires" was solved.

Eternal granite hewn from the living isle
And dowelled with brute iron,
Rears a tower that from its wet foundation
To its crown of glittering glass,
Stands, in the sweep of winds,
Immovable, immortal, eminent.

Robert Louis Stevenson

CAPE FLORIDA, FLA.
(Key Biscayne)

HISTORY. Florida became a territory of the U.S. in 1821. The coast in that area had been claiming ships since the discovery of the area in 1497 by John Cabot. The Federal Government was in the process of building a string of lighthouses on the Atlantic Coast, and so added one for Cape Florida. Samuel B. Lincoln built a 65 foot tower of bricks, with walls five feet thick at the base, tapering off to two feet at the top. It was not until later that it was discovered that the builder had cheated on his contract, in that he had made the walls hollow instead of solid, thus saving half of the brick he was supposed to use. The lighthouse was completed in 1825, and is one of the oldest structures in Florida.

The lighthouse was partially destroyed in an Indian attack in 1836 (see below) and was finally repaired in 1846.

In 1855, during a period of peace, the height of the tower was increased from 65 to 95 feet, and a fresnel lens was installed.

Once again, in 1861, the lighthouse was put out of commission by force, by a band of Confederates and was relit in 1867.

The light was taken out of service in 1878, when the Fowey Rock Light (located two miles southeast of Key Biscayne) was lit. However, once again this historic light

47

showed its ability to bounce back. One hundred years later, on July 4, 1978, the light was reinstalled by the coast guard. It again provides light, fulfilling its destiny.

MUSEUM OR INTERPRETIVE SERVICE.   This lighthouse is one of the lucky ones. Looked after by the Florida Department of Natural Resources, it is a part of the Bill Baggs Cape Florida State Recreation Area. The lighthouse and a replica of the keeper's house and out-buildings are maintained in an area that also has native plants once common on Key Biscayne along the trails. Guided tours are conducted daily except Tuesday, at 10:30, 1:00, 2:30 and 3:30. There are 121 steps to the top of the lighthouse, and you can inspect a fine example of a fresnel lens in the lantern room at the top. The view is a fine one. There is also a beach and picnic area within sight.

GETTING THERE.   From I-95 take the exit marked 26th Rd. heading for Rickenbacker Causeway ($1.00 toll). Cross the causeway, and stay on Crandon Blvd. on Key Biscayne to its end, which will be the entrance to the park. There is a small fee for entry to the park. Obtain a map from the gatekeeper, and follow the main road to the lighthouse site.

TALES AND LEGENDS.   On July 23, 1836 this lighthouse and the men who were guarding it at the time underwent one of the severest ordeals of all, an Indian siege. The assistant keeper, John B. Thompson and his helper barely made it to the lighthouse after sighting the Seminole attackers. They barricaded themselves in the lighthouse and held off the Indians with gunfire. The Seminoles soon set fire to the wooden door and window, forcing the two men, both wounded, to climb to the top of the lighthouse and, to escape the fire, fed by 225 gallons of oil stored in the tower, they moved out onto the two feet wide platform. As the intensity of the fire increased the men were in danger of being roasted alive. Thompson, his oil soaked clothing aflame, threw a keg of gunpowder down the lighthouse steps. The resulting explosion, instead of killing the men, temporarily dampened the fire, but did not put it out. Just as Thompson was about to give up and jump to his death, the burning steps collapsed, lessening the heat, and a welcome breeze came in from the ocean, cooling the tormented man. His companion had fallen to a rifle ball a short time before. The Indians, after looting the keeper's house, left him for dead, taking his sloop. The crew of a navy ship, the U.S.S. Motto, heard the explosion, and came to the site with his sloop in tow. They struggled to get a rope to the wounded man, finally firing a ramrod with a string attached, to enable a rope and pulley to be raised to the tower and Assistant Keeper Thompson, with three bullet wounds in each foot and severe burns over much of his body, lived to serve another day.

A Fine Example of A Fresnel Lens

KEY WEST, FLA.

HISTORY. The first lighthouse on Key West was built on Whitehead Point in 1825. The 65 foot tower was destroyed in 1846, by a hurricane that killed the keeper and his family. A 65 foot tower, built away from the beach, was completed in 1847, and was made 20 feet higher in 1894, to a total of 85 feet, which being 14 feet above sea level, made the tower 100 feet above sea level. It burned whale oil, then was electrified and automated, and was taken out of service in 1969.

MUSEUM OR INTERPRETIVE SERVICE. When the lighthouse was taken out of service, the Key West Art and Historical Society got the future use of it as a part of a museum complex which houses military and marine artifacts in the old keeper's house, as well as a Japanese two-man submarine, a TF-9 Cougar airplane and other weapons in the yard. The periscope from a submarine that was stationed at Key West affords a fine view of the city. The museum is open every day but Christmas from 9:30 to 5:00. Admission is $2.00.

GETTING THERE. Take U.S. Rt. 1 into Key West, continuing on North Roosevelt Blvd. to Truman Ave. to Whitehead St. The complex is on the corner to your right. As you drive down Rte. 1 over the keys, keep a lookout to your left, where you can spot some of the offshore "Reef Lights" in the distance.

TALES AND LEGENDS. None now known.

DRY TORTUGAS, FLA.

HISTORY. This is actually a history of two lighthouses. The first one, called the Dry Tortugas (Sea Turtle) Lighthouse was built on Bush Key (later renamed Garden Key) in 1825. This light served until the U.S. Army built Fort Jefferson on the key. The old tower was moved onto the battlements of the fort and was used as a harbor light for Tortugas Harbor, later the home of the "Great White Squadron." The flagship of the squadron was the Battleship Maine, which was sunk in Havana harbor to bring on the Spanish-American War. Fort Jefferson was also made famous by one of its major prisoners, Dr. Samuel Mudd, who was unjustly accused of conspiracy in the shooting of President Lincoln.

LIGHTHOUSE-
FT. JEFFERSON

In 1858 the Lighthouse Board had a new tower built on Loggerhead Key, within sight of Garden Key. The first order lens were moved from Garden Key, and the new lighthouse, 151 feet above sea level, was operable. This light, which is still active, is sometimes referred to as the Loggerhead Key Lighthouse.

The Loggerhead Key Lighthouse was damaged in the hurricane of 1873. The Lighthouse board asked for and received the money for a new tower. However, after repairing the old tower, and seeing how it withstood another hurricane soon after, the Board abandoned plans for a new one. The light, which now has a second order lens, can be seen for 28 miles. It is brick, painted half white and half black.

LOGGERHEAD
KEY LIGHT-
AIR VIEW

51

MUSEUM OR INTERPRETIVE SERVICE. There was very little information on the lighthouses themselves, but there is a great deal of historical interest in Fort Jefferson itself, which is maintained by the National Park Service. An unspoiled beach and a sea turtle nursery add to the pleasure of a visit there.

GETTING THERE. There is reportedly a boat ride to Fort Jefferson, but the boat was out of service when we visited. I had the pleasure of flying to Fort Jefferson in a seaplane, which allowed me to stay on the island for half of the day. During the thirty minute flight, the pilot flew low enough to see a manta ray, some sharks, and the outlines of two sunken ships. Then he was good enough to fly around Loggerhead Key so that I could take some pictures. The Key West Seaplane Service provided the flight (305) 294–6978.

TALES AND LEGENDS. None available on the lighthouses. There are two interesting tales about Fort Jefferson. One, the guns of this great fort were never fired in battle, perhaps since no enemy came close enough. A second story tells of the heroism of Dr. Mudd in a yellow fever epidemic that swept the fort, immediately killing the fort's medical personnel. Dr. Mudd labored heroically to save the lives of the men of the fort.

The rocky ledge runs far into the sea,
And on its outer point, some miles away,
The lighthouse lifts its massive masonry.

Longfellow

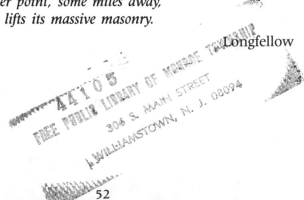

GLOSSARY OF TERMS

Argand lamp—A lamp designed by swiss chemist Aimé Argand. The lamp had a cylindrical wick supplied with air within as well as without to expose a maximum of air to the fuel.

candlepower—luminous intensity of a light expressed in candles.

classification of lens—Lenses are classified as to size by the term "order", the first order being the largest and the sixth order being the smallest. The actual size of the lens is measured at its inside diameter. The following is a list of the standard lenses:

ORDER	INSIDE DIAMETER	HEIGHT
First	72^{7}/$_{16}$ inches	7 ft. 10 in.
Second	55^{1}/$_{8}$ inches	6 ft. 1 in.
Third	39^{3}/$_{8}$ inches	4 ft. 8 in.
Fourth	19^{11}/$_{16}$ inches	2 ft. 4 in.
Fifth	14^{3}/$_{4}$ inches	1 ft. 8 in.
Sixth	11^{3}/$_{4}$ inches	1 ft. 5 in.

(The information above was obtained from "Historically Famous Lighthouses", Coast Guard Publication #232, U.S. Government Printing Office, 1972.)

encroachment—the act of advancing or making inroads beyond the usual limits.

fresnel lens—a lens designed by physicist August Fresnel in 1822. The lens concentrated light rays, and greatly improved the visibility of lighthouses.

lantern room—the glassed-in enclosure at the top of a lighthouse which surrounds and protects the lens.

lighthouse leg—an extreme stiffness felt in the front of the thighs the day after climbing to the top of a lighthouse and back down. Not experienced by young people, or those who are used to it.

nominal range—the distance from which a light can be seen on a clear night from the bridge of a ship 30 feet high.

parabolic reflector—A reflector with a curved shape, designed to concentrate light rays into a single beam.

prism—a device for bending (refracting) or concentrating light, as in a lens.

spermaceti—a white waxy substance separated from the oil contained in the head of a sperm whale. Used for candles.

spider lamp—a lamp with a number of wicks protruding from a single reservoir.

tabby—a building material made of equal parts of lime, shells and gravel. Was used in coastal areas for building.

wickie—term historically used to refer to lighthouse keepers. Current use refers to both keepers and supporters.

SELECTED GENERAL REFERENCES

Adamson, Hans Christian, "Keepers of the Lights," Greenberg Publishers, N.Y., 1955.

Beaver, Patrick, "A History of Lighthouses", Peter Davies Publishers, London, 1971.

Holland, Francis Ross, Jr., "America's Lighthouses: Their Illustrated History Since 1716", The Stephen Green Press, Brattleboro, Vt., 1972.

Nordhoff, Charles (ed.), "The Lighthouses of The United States in 1874", Outbooks, Golden, Colorado, 1981.

Stevenson, David Alan, "The World's Lighthouses Before 1820", Oxford University Press, London, 1959.

U.S. Coast Guard, "Historically Famous Lighthouses", CG 232, Department of Transportation, U.S. Government Printing Office, Washington, 1972.

LIGHTHOUSE SOCIETIES AND ASSOCIATIONS

(Send for membership applications.)

The United States Lighthouse Society
130 St. Elmo Way
San Francisco, California 94127

A non-profit historical and educational organization dealing with matters of interest concerning the lighthouses of the United States. Publishes "Keeper's Log", a quarterly magazine about lighthouses and the technology and people associated with them now and in the past.

Great Lakes Lighthouse Keepers Association
P.O. Box 2907
Southfield, Michigan 48037

An organization with similar objectives to the above organization, except that interest is limited to the lighthouses of the Great Lakes. Publishes a quarterly newsletter "The Beacon".

Ponce DeLeon Inlet Lighthouse Preservation Association, Inc.
4931 South Peninsula Drive
Ponce Inlet, Florida 32019

A non-profit historical association that has preserved and restored the lighthouse and keepers buildings and established a museum there. The Association sends out periodic newsletters.

Coastal Georgia Historical Society
P.O. Box 1151
St. Simons Island, Georgia 31522

A non-profit historical society that has established and operates the Museum of Coastal History on St. Simons Island and has responsibility for visitors to the lighthouse, which, is open to the public at specified times. The Society also puts out publications.

Tybee Museum Association
P.O. Box 1334
Tybee Island, Georgia 31328

This association runs the Tybee Museum across from Tybee Light in Georgia.

Key West Art and Historical Society
938 Whitehead St.
Key West, Florida 33040

This association maintains and operates the Lighthouse and Military Museum and the East Martello Gallery and Museum in Key West, Florida.

Loxahatchee Historical Society, Inc.
P.O. Box 1506
Jupiter, Florida 33458

This society maintains and operates a museum within view of the Jupiter Inlet lighthouse, with area history, including lighthouse materials.

INDEX